~ POSTCARDS FROM

OLD BEBINGTON

Dave Mitchelson

Copyright © D. Mitchelson, 1989, 1998

All Rights Reserved. No part of this publication may be reproduced, stored in a retrieval system, or transmitted in any form or by any means – electronic, mechanical, photocopying, recording, or otherwise – without prior written permission from the publisher.

First published in 1991 as "Old Bebington: a portrait in photographs and old picture postcards" by S.B. Publications

This fully revised edition is published by Sigma Leisure – an imprint of Sigma Press, 1 South Oak Lane, Wilmslow, Cheshire SK9 6AR, England.

British Library Cataloguing in Publication Data
A CIP record for this book is available from the British Library.

ISBN: 1-85058-669-1

Typesetting and Design by: Sigma Press, Wilmslow, Cheshire.

Cover photograph: Eastham Pier, c. 1910

CONTENTS

Acknowledgements v
Foreword vi
The Author vii
Introduction .... vii-x
Map x
Comic Card 1
Bebington Coat of Arms 2

NEW FERRY

An aerial view 3
The Beach 4-5
The Pier 6-8
The Training Ships 9-10
New Ferry Hotel 11
The Ferry Approach 12
Multiview of New Ferry 13
Great Eastern Hotel 14
The Isolation Hospital 15-16
The Brickworks 17
The Open-Air Baths 18
New Ferry Road 19-20
The Toll Bar 21
The Lyceum, New Chester Road 22
The Park 23-24
Bebington Road 25-26

BEBINGTON

The Oval 27
Avro 504K at Bebington 28
Townfield Lane 29
The Village 30-31
Acres Road 32
The Village 33
Bebington Old Hall 34
St. Andrew's Church 35
Church Road 36
The Roman Road 37
Footpath to Higher Bebington 38

HIGHER BEBINGTON

Kings Yard 39
Christchurch 40
Old Cottage 41
Victoria Hall 42
Cheirotherium 43
The Great Cutting 44
The Cross Roads, Mount Road 45
Storeton Quarries 46
Butlers Farm 47
Mount Road 48
Needwood Farm 49

VILLAGES

Brimstage	50
The Stores, Thornton Hough	51
All Saints Church, Thornton Hough	52
Wheatsheaf Inn, Raby	53
Raby Mere	54-55

BROMBOROUGH

Dibbinsdale	56-57
Rustic bridge in the Woods	58
Allport Road	59
Knockaloe Lodge	60

EASTHAM

Plymyard House	61
The Post Office	62
Carlett Cottages	63
Greenwood Tea-Rooms	64
The Ferry	65-66
The Ship Canal	67
The Ferry Hotel	68
The Pleasure Gardens	69-72
Job's Ferry	73
The Woods	74

BROMBOROUGH

Mendell House	75
The Village	76
The Cross	77
Village Road	78
Bromborough Hall	79-80
Stanhope House	81
Spital Road	82-83
Dibbin Bridge	84
Spital Dam	85
The Magazine Ship	86
Bromborough Pool School	87
Bromborough Dock	88

PORT SUNLIGHT

Multiview	89

NEW FERRY

New Chester Road School	90
New Chester Road	91
Mrs Smith's Shop	92
The Toll Bar	93

S.B. Publications	94

ACKNOWLEDGEMENTS

The author would like to thank all those who have helped him with research, loan of postcards and photographs for this book:
Bebington Reference Library;
Ian Boumphrey;
Phil Carson;
Tony Edwards;
Jack and Bill Fairs;
Ivy Forsyth;
Gerry and Dot Froggett;
Mike Gibbons;
Gillian Jackson;
Gerald Mottershead;
Glyn Parry;
Miss Thelwall.
Gillian Jackson for editing the text; Steve Benz for additional editing and marketing.

FOREWORD

What occurs to us local lads of long ago, as we linger over Dave Mitchelson's careful descriptions and evocative assemblage of photographs in his first and, now, in this his second collection, is how visible were the lives lived locally in the first part of this century. It was possible to see where and how the wealthy lived, how businesses and trades were conducted and how ordinary families found enjoyment nearby on their scarce days off.

Yet, no development without change, it is said. Social conditions are not so very less harsh. One time luxuries are now considered to be everyday necessities. But Dave's enthusiasm for the past is soundly based; it serves to alert us to how much we lose as well as gain when scientific progress allows us to dwell so privately, travel so individually, work so invisibly and be entertained so electronically.

A Wirral peninsula covered only by roads; houses; shopping precincts; science and business parks; industrial estates; hotel, sports, hospital and educational complexes, would be a very alienating place indeed. We must certainly strive to preserve something to remind our descendants of the way we used to LIVE! In future there may be lessons to be learnt about scale and pace, simple pleasures and free opportunity for social contact.

Thank you, Dave

Jack and Bill Fairs
April, 1991

THE AUTHOR

Dave Mitchelson (1937 - 1994) was born in Rock Ferry, where he lived for all his life.

For almost forty years, Dave was a supporter of nature conservation. For a number of years, he was a Park Ranger for Wirral Borough Council and was a leader and guide on local history walks. His special interests were butterflies and wild flowers and, over the years, he built up a large photographic library on these subjects. In more recent years, he also amassed a large collection of slides and photographs of local history and became a founder member of the Wirral Postcard Club. He used his extensive photographic library in illustrated talks.

Dave Mitchelson also compiled *Postcards from the Past: Rock Ferry, New Ferry and Bebington*, republished in 1998 by Sigma Leisure.

INTRODUCTION

Since the publication of my last book — *Rock Ferry, New Ferry and Bebington — A Portrait in Old Picture Postcards* — I have been inundated with requests for a book on Bebington, covering all districts of the old borough — "so this is it!"

The Borough of Bebington has only been in existence since 1937, when a Charter of Incorporation was granted and the new coat of arms was used. The early history of the area we now know as Bebington is poorly documented. However, I believe that the name is of Saxon origin; Bebba was probably a Saxon chief and ton meant the home of. Bebington was not mentioned in the Domesday Book but several of the surrounding villages are: Eastham is listed as 'Estham', the landholder being Earl Hugh, with a mill; Poulton is 'Pontone', landholder Richard Butler, and was a hamlet; Raby is 'Rabie', landholder St. Werburgh's Church, and was a village; Storeton is 'Stortone', landholder Nigel de Burcy, a village, and Thornton Hough is 'Torintone', landholder William from Robert of Rhuddlan, a village.

For more than a thousand years, the area has been a patchwork of small villages and hamlets, all playing their own part in the area's history. Storeton was once the home of Alan Sylvester, Wirral's first forester and originator of the 'Wirral Horn', in 1100 A.D. I wonder how many readers have heard of Shodwell village? It once stood on the fringe of Eastham Woods, on the banks of the River Mersey. I believe that the name is a corruption of 'St. Chad's Well'. A well was found on the site of what is now Bromborough Power Station.

Because of the limitations of space for text, it has been difficult to include all the information that I would have liked to write about. However, I feel that the pictures tell a thousand stories. For many of these pictures, we are indebted to the local and national photographers, whose firms published their photographs as postcards — for all to see. Particular mention should be made of George Davies who had offices in Port Sunlight and New Ferry. There is hardly a corner of the borough that was not captured by his camera and, since many of these views have changed beyond all recognition, they provide a valuable record of our local history.

Picture postcards were first used in this country in the 1890s. These early cards were known as 'court cards' and were much smaller than the standard size that was adopted just before the turn of the century. All these early cards had small pictures on the front with a space for correspondence, while the back was reserved for the address. In 1902, the 'divided back' postcard was introduced, so that both the message and address could be written on the back and the front used entirely for a picture. At about this time, postcard collecting became an international craze and an album of cards was a feature of many homes — this explains why so many Edwardian postcards bear the simple message 'Another for your album'.

Between 1902 and 1918, millions of postcards were published annually. As well as being saved by collectors, they were a cheap and convenient method of communication. Encouraged by a ½d. postage rate and several postal deliveries and collections a day, cards were used for domestic and business correspondence, for advertising purposes and, in the absence of newspaper pictures, were sometimes the best visual record of national and local events.

After World War I, the postage rate was increased to 1d. and the telephone replaced the postcard as a convenient form of communication. As a result, sales of postcards decreased and were mainly of the picturesque type, sent by people on holiday. Today, as at the beginning of the century, a vast range of postcards is available and postcard collecting is an international hobby, second only to stamp collecting in popularity.

In the early 1900s, Bebington was well-illustrated on postcards but, in later years, because it is not a resort area, there were only a few views available. However, I feel that the residents of Bebington are fortunate to be living in this area. On the coast there is the Mersey and, inland, there is some wonderful countryside. We have three of the finest wooded areas in Wirral: Eastham, Dibbinsdale and Storeton. We also have golf courses, football pitches, country parks, nature reserves, urban parks and a large leisure complex — the Oval.

I hope you enjoy this book and that it brings back happy memories for some readers. Perhaps it will help us to realise that 'the future must learn from the past'.

Dave Mitchelson
February, 1991

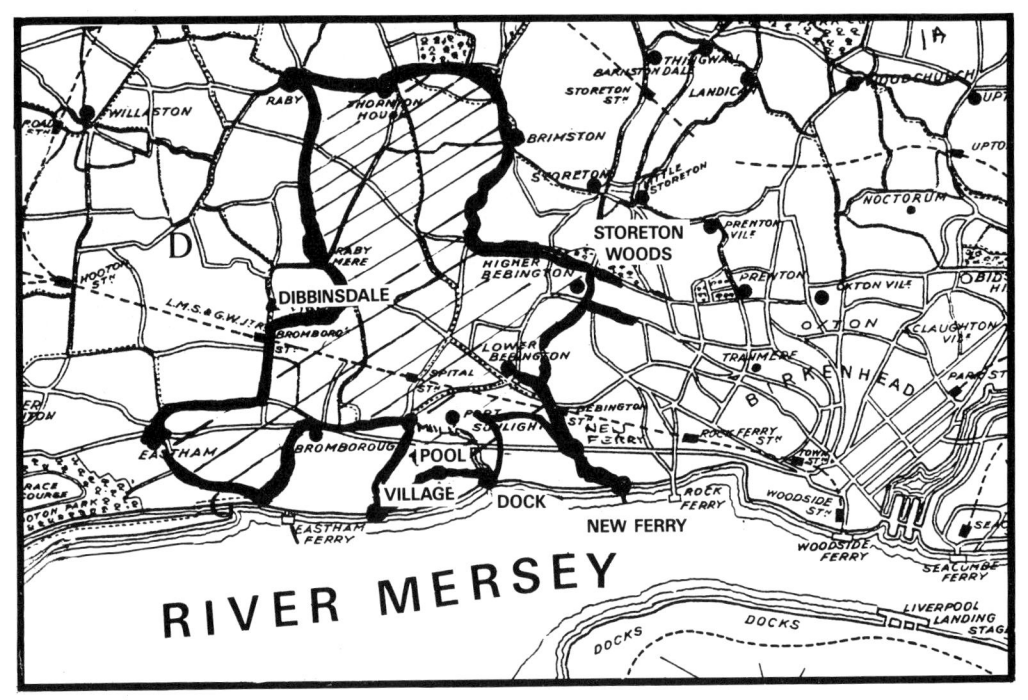

THE ROUTE

The sequence of cards has been arranged to follow the route of a 'walk' — albeit a long one! Starting at the old pier area of New Ferry, it leads to Lower Bebington Village and on up to Higher Bebington, through Storeton Woods, past the quarries and Needwood. Next are the outlying villages of Brimstage, Thornton Hough and Raby, and on down the lanes to Raby Mere and Dibbinsdale. From here, we enter Bromborough and Eastham, before crossing the A41 to Eastham Village, the ferry and Eastham Woods. The route then leads to Bromborough Village, Brotherton Park and Spital Dam before crossing the A41 again for Magazine Village and Bromborough Pool and Dock.
Finally, we return inland to Port Sunlight and finish at the Toll Bar in New Ferry.

COMIC CARD FROM ROCK FERRY

To start this book I would like to use this comic postcard to say 'Greetings!' from an old Rock Ferryite!

I hope that you will enjoy this book which is based on the old Borough of Bebington, which became part of Wirral Borough, after the reorganisation of boundaries in 1974.

From a Gay Dog at Rock Ferry

THE COAT OF ARMS OF BEBINGTON URBAN DISTRICT COUNCIL

The Coat of Arms was granted to the Borough, by the King of Arms, in 1934. In heraldic terms the shield has a per chevron azure and or in chief, a saltire couped argent between two garbs or and, in base, a lymphad sail-furled sable, flags flying to the dexter gules. (The silver cross is for St. Andrew's and the gold wheatsheaves are for Cheshire.) The crest has a representation of Bromborough Cross in front of a rising golden sun, laid on a wreath of blue and gold. The motto 'Civitatis Fortuna Cives' means 'the fortune of the state depends upon the citizens'.

AERIAL VIEW OF NEW FERRY, c. 1920
From the air, the pier can be seen in all its glory. On the shore, the Ferry Office, Esplanade and New Ferry Hotel can all be clearly identified, with 'the Gap' just below them. It is roughly at this point where the area known as New Ferry begins and, so, from here we start on our walking tour around the 'old Borough of Bebington'.

THE BEACH, NEW FERRY, c. 1931
This view of 'the Gap', at the bottom of the Dell, shows Dell Cottage, which housed a gate-keeper, whose job it was to prevent unauthorised entry in to the Barton Estate. This Estate consisted of four large villas in The Dell, four in Rock Park Road and two cottages in Delta Road. The large villas on the left of this view were Scott's Villa and Dean House. These were destroyed by the Luftwaffe during the blitz of World War 2. Dell Cottage was pulled down in the mid-1960s. Modern houses and flats now occupy the site.

BEACH & CONWAY (TRAINING SHIP), NEW FERRY.   No KNF2

THE BEACH AND THE 'CONWAY', NEW FERRY, c. 1935

The Gap was a favourite play area for the children of The Dell and from the surrounding areas. The sand was always clean and the water was free from pollution — unlike today. This view shows children enjoying themselves with the building of sandcastles. On the left is the start of the Promenade which runs along the riverbank to Rock Ferry. It was at this point that a pill-box was built during World War 2; it was removed in the late 1970s. In the background, the famous *Conway* training ship can be seen. (see page 9)

Entrance to Pier, New Ferry.

ENTRANCE TO THE PIER, NEW FERRY, c. 1909

Taken from the Promenade, this view clearly shows the Ferry Office, Esplanade houses and New Ferry Hotel. The ferry service was closed in 1922, but the office buildings remained until the early 1950s. To the right of the ferry office, in this picture, is the house that was once owned by Mr. Lamey, a tug boat owner and a very well-known local resident. Through the trees on the right, stands the majestic New Ferry Hotel. The ferry, trees and hotel have all gone and remain only as memories.

NEW FERRY PIER, c. 1913

The ferry was opened in 1865 and provided an excellent and well-patronised service until 1897, when Birkenhead Corporation took over the running of the ferries. From this time, it was operated at a loss because of the increasing popularity of the railway system. In 1922, a drunken, Dutch captain rammed his steamer into the end of the pier, wrecking the pontoon which floated away down the river, between the *Indefatigable* and the *Conway*. The boys from the *Conway* lowered longboats and secured the pontoon to Rock Ferry pier. As a direct result of the accident, the ferry service was closed down and, in 1929, the pier was demolished.

NEW FERRY PIER, c. 1912

Looking back along the pier to the shore, this view shows the Esplanade, the New Ferry Hotel and the Ferry Office. In the foreground, one of the boys from the training ship *Indefatigable* is posing for the photographer; this young lad cannot be more than 13-years-old. The pier was built in 1865. It was constructed of both iron and steel and its iron supports were sunk some 20ft into the bed of the river. It had a double walkway with cement surfaces and was the longest pier on the Mersey, stretching almost 850ft. into the river. Of the eight ferry landing stages that were built along the Mersey, only three remain: Rock Ferry, Seacombe and Woodside.

THE TRAINING SHIPS, c. 1904

For the past 200 years, many a fine ship has been associated with the River Mersey. However, not many were as well-known as the four training ships — the wooden walls of England. The ships were the *Akbar,* moored in 1856, the *Conway,* 1859, the *Indefatigable,* 1864, and the *Clarence,* 1864. From the left, this view shows the *Conway, Akbar* and *Indi* moored off Rock Ferry and New Ferry. The *Clarence* was set on fire and destroyed in 1889.

THE 'INDEFATIGABLE', c. 1934

The first *Indi* was brought to the Mersey in 1864, and was made ready to receive boys in the training of seamanship. These boys were either orphans or from families of 'poor circumstance'. The ship was moored close to the prestigious training ship *Conway,* for a short time. The Conway Association complained about this proximity and the *Indi* was moved to New Ferry. In 1914, the old ship was replaced by the *Phaeton,* whose name was changed to *Indefatigable*. This ship — pictured here — lasted until 1941, when it was towed away to the breakers yard. The Indi Association is still running today, and is based on Anglesey.

NEW FERRY HOTEL, c. 1900

The first building on this site was a small cottage, about which no information has yet been found. The building shown here is the second hotel, which was built about 1896-98. It is said that Queen Victoria had a drink here when she visited the area. In the early years of the twentieth century, various extensions were added, transforming the hotel to the building that is fondly remembered by older residents. (see next page) The hotel and pier were once owned by R. A. Macfie. The hotel was demolished in the 1970s but, in its place, stands Derwent Court, a residential home; one of the finest of its kind, with splendid views of the river.

THE FERRY APPROACH, NEW FERRY, c. 1906

This postcard gives us some idea of the heritage that has been lost. The hotel, built in the late 1890s, has gone; the ferry and pier, opened in 1865, have gone and the shops, opened in 1867, have closed and are now flats. This loss is repeated throughout the borough; approximately 90% of the views shown in this book are no longer there — gone without a trace.

MULTIVIEW OF NEW FERRY, c. 1934

Multiview postcards were very popular as they showed several views of the area one lived in or were visiting. Clockwise, from the top left, this postcard shows: New Ferry Park Lodge; New Ferry Hotel and approach to the ferry; the Hotel from the ferry; The Dell and, in the centre, the training ship *Indefatigable*.

THE GREAT EASTERN HOTEL, NEW FERRY, c. 1912

This fine old Hotel in New Ferry Road was named after Brunel's famous ship of the same name, which was dismantled on New Ferry shore. The ship's artefacts were auctioned and a number of these were bought and fitted into the Hotel. The bar and a beautiful stained glass window, depicting the old ship, can still be seen, with permission from the landlord. Visitors today — as 150 years ago — are made very welcome at the 'Eastern' — the manager being very proud of his hotel.

THE NURSES' HOME

THE ISOLATION HOSPITAL, NEW FERRY, c. 1900

In the mid-nineteenth century, there were no fewer than ten quarantine ships moored in the river to cater for people with tropical diseases — cholera being the cause of the most deaths. The ships proved to be inadequate and it was decided to erect a purpose-built hospital in New Ferry, overlooking the river. In 1875, the hospital was opened. It had very high forbidding walls and consisted of several wards, a laundry and houses for nurses and doctors — shown in this view. At the base of the cliffs, stood another wall topped by a high metal fence. Set into this wall was a single gate which was kept locked .... (see next page)

THE JETTY

THE JETTY, THE ISOLATION HOSPITAL, NEW FERRY, c. 1900
....From the gate, jutting out into the river, a long wooden jetty was constructed to run out to low water. It was along this jetty that the patients suffering from tropical diseases were brought ashore. Over 1,200 cases of tropical diseases including cholera, smallpox, chickenpox, even leprosy were treated at the hospital. During the 88 years that it stood on the clifftop, the hospital received little recognition — its moment of glory yet to come. In 1963, it was burnt to the ground by the Fire Department; the flames could be seen licking the sky from as far away as Runcorn. No trace of the hospital can be found today.

NEW FERRY BRICKWORKS, c. 1914

The Brickworks were situated on the banks of the Mersey, in an area known as Mayfields. The work must have been hard and the pay poor. In this picture, the boy on the right and the young man in the centre both have bare feet. The large chimney stack — behind the boy on the right — was demolished in 1924. The small one in the distance was at Beaconsfield Road Brickworks. On the left of the picture, there is a mountain made up of thousands of bricks; these would have been distributed by barge, around the Wirral coastline. This spot is now occupied by a large, modern effluent plant, run and owned by the Water Authority.

The Bath, New Ferry.

THE SWIMMING BATHS, NEW FERRY, c. 1935
This view brings back many happy memories for me! This super pool was 330ft long, 90ft wide, with a depth sloping from 3ft to 16ft. No matter how many came, there was always room for everyone. If the changing rooms were full, bathers changed behind their towels and left their clothes in the park — they were always there when they returned. There was also a small café with watered-down soft drinks and burnt ice cream, many wonderful trees to climb, and grass banks that were ideal for sunbathing, I caught sunstroke there when I was 12-years-old! How many readers recall 'bunking' into the baths over the hospital wall? A housing estate stands on the site today.

OLD COTTAGES, NEW FERRY ROAD, c. 1914

These cottages adjoined the Travellers Rest public house. They were built in the 1870s and, for the next few years, were occupied by the employees of the brickworks. In 1906, a few cottages were pulled down to make room for 'Hope Hall', a small church that still stands today. In 1934, an extension was added to the hall. The cottages in the picture fell into disrepair and were pulled down in the 1950s. Part of the site is now occupied by the car park for the Travellers Rest, with advertising hoardings occupying the remaining space.

THE TRAVELLERS REST, NEW FERRY ROAD, c. 1915
The ivy-draped Travellers Rest still stands on the corner of Marquis Street. It is thought that the inn opened in circa 1860 and the landlord — or lady — was Eliza Leay. I have been told that the inn was a one-room establishment until the cottage next door was acquired and incorporated with the inn to make it larger. This view seems to confirm these facts. At the time, the inn served West Cheshire Brewery Ales and the licensee was also a dealer in tobacco. It is still a popular public house and is known locally as 'Smokies'. The ivy, along with the cottages, has gone.

THE TOLL BAR, NEW FERRY, c. 1922

Probably the best-known part of New Ferry, the Toll Bar has been the focal point since its introduction in 1844. At that time, the area was known as 'The Pasture', but when the pier and ferry were opened, in 1865, it became New Ferry. This view was taken from Bebington Road, looking down New Ferry Road to the Travellers Rest. At the busy junction, there is the familiar figure of a policeman on point duty. On the right, above the doorway, there seems to be a carved beehive and, above it, the date 1855, with the initials C. M. which stand for Charles Morris, baker and grocer. In 1876, David Edwards, beer seller and cow keeper, lived at No 17 — The Wynnstay Hotel.

THE LYCEUM, NEW CHESTER ROAD, NEW FERRY, February 1915

The Lyceum Picture House — 'the flea pit' — was a great place to visit, along with the Palace and Rialto, (see page 26). It was opened in August, 1913, with the film 'The Lighthouse Prisoners'. In the heyday of the 'pictures', we were able to go and watch those wonderful stars like John Wayne, Alan Ladd and Robert Mitchum. I can remember queuing for three nights to see John Wayne in 'Red River' — I never did get in! This view shows the 'Bantams' regiment at a halt; a vicar can be seen in the centre of the group. The men were probably on their way to the docks, to be shipped over to France. The Lyceum closed in 1962, and the site is now occupied by a Kwik Save Supermarket.

THE LODGE, NEW FERRY PARK, c. 1922

The Lodge once guarded the main entrance to New Ferry Park. The two large gates, one on either side of the lodge, were locked every night and the park patrolled by the park keeper. All the way around the building, between the two storeys, there is an inscription which reads: 'Erected A.D. M.D.C.C.C.I.V. and presented to the Lower Bebington Urban District Council by W. H. Lever Esq.' I wonder what he would think if he could see the state of it today?

THE BOWLING GREEN, NEW FERRY PARK, c. 1934
When I was a child, this park was a lovely place. The bowling green, in particular, stands out in my memory. It had banked sides with benches around it, and a pavilion with roses growing all over it. Also in the park, there was a garden for the blind, with highly-scented flowers and braille name plates next to them. The residents lost more than the bowling greens when the area became part of Wirral Borough Council — they lost everything.

BEBINGTON ROAD, NEW FERRY, c. 1922

Looking towards the Toll Bar, this view shows the fine church that stood on the corner of Boundary Road. It had an ageing notice that read: 'CH--CH — what is missing — UR'; sadly, it was demolished in the 1960s. The Co-op. food store and undertakers occupied part of the site. All the buildings on the left are still standing but the shops have changed hands. Familiar names from the 1940s, 50s and 60s are: 'Bon-Ton' gown shop; Gregorys' ladies and childrens' wear; Heggs shoe repairs and Mr. O'Brian, an optician. On the left, beside the two gentlemen, stands an unusual road sign — 'Dangerous crossing drive slowly'. This section of the road is now pedestrianised.

THE RIALTO, BEBINGTON ROAD, c. 1933
Situated in Bebington Road, not far from the railway station, this cinema opened in July, 1933, in competition with the Lyceum (see page 22). At that time, the Rialto was one of the most up-to-date cinemas in Wirral and people came from near and far to queue for seats. This continued for most nights throughout the 1940s and 1950s as well. In 1961, it showed its last film and closed down. The building was then used as a furniture store but is now a snooker club.

WIRRAL AGRICULTURAL SHOW GROUNDS, BEBINGTON.

"The Unique Series."

WIRRAL AGRICULTURAL SHOW GROUNDS, BEBINGTON, c. 1906
These show grounds are now known as The Oval. The entrance and stands are still there, but the cowsheds, fields, donkeys and footpath to Barlow Avenue have gone. During World War 1, The Oval was used as an army camp and training ground and the cowsheds became billets for the troops. In 1919, Levers bought the grounds and, in 1966, it was taken over by Cheshire County Council. The Oval is now owned by Wirral Borough Council. Scenes from the award-winning film 'Chariots of Fire' were filmed here, where a large model of Columbea stadium was built, to simulate the Paris Olympics of 1924.

AVRO 504K AT THE OVAL, c. 1932

Aeroplanes like this were a familiar sight on the Wirral in the 1920s and 30s. Gerald Mottershead remembers this plane and pilot very well. They were used by Cobham's Circus which visited the fields at the rear of The Oval, where this picture was taken. The 1918 vintage plane was owned by the North British Aviation Company who were based at Hooton Park. The pilot was Captain William McKay, who autographed this card, and is shown in the inset picture. For a fee of 5/- a flight, he would take off with his passenger, and Gerald and other intrepid people were able to view the Wirral from the air. Captain McKay was killed during a flying display in 1934.

TOWNFIELD LANE, BEBINGTON, c. 1930

The picture shows nothing more than a country lane — a far cry from what it is today! Most of the trees have gone and only a short section of the wall remains. The lane was once used for herding cattle, sheep and pigs to graze on fields now occupied by The Oval, Bebington Cemetery and various housing estates. When walking along the lane all those years ago, one would have passed large homes belonging to the gentry — such as 'Richmond Hill', 'Wellington Park' and 'The Oaklands'. The first two houses have long since been pulled down to make way for modern houses — all that remains are their names on the new road signs. Stonehill Park was another area that the lane ran past; this is now covered by Stonehill Avenue and Barlow Avenue.

THE VILLAGE, BEBINGTON, c. 1935
This postcard, together with five others, was commissioned by John Klink of 14, The Village. They were sold exclusively in his shop which can be seen in this view, next to Irwins' grocery. Apart from the addition of a pavement on the left-hand side, a change of ownership at the shops and the loss of Bebington Old Hall, the scene is almost unchanged. Shops like Irwins and the Co-op were the forerunners of today's supermarkets. How many readers can remember shopping at these stores — buying ¼lb of tea and sugar mix, sold in a brown paper bag, or a cob of butter that would be taken from a barrel on the counter? The Environmental Health Department would not approve of such practices today!

THATCHED COTTAGES. — LOWER BEBINGTON.

THE THATCHED COTTAGE, THE VILLAGE, BEBINGTON, c. 1910

The cottage was built in c. 1656 and is known locally as 'The Thatch'. Until the local council sold it, a few years ago, it was the oldest council house in Wirral. On the left is The Grove, showing a house that still stands today. When the road was re-routed in 1840, the Grove became a backwater where time has stood still — walking there today is just as it was a century ago. The main feature that is missing is the large house called 'Laurel Bank'. This was used as a college for some years — until Carlett Park was built — and was pulled down in the 1960s when the site became part of Mayer Park. The small gate-house to 'Laurel Bank' still stands.

ACRES ROAD, BEBINGTON
c. 1912

I have included this postcard because I like it and feel that it has historical significance. 'The Acres' was a large house that stood a little way down from Higher Bebington Road. The gatepost of the house is on the left of this picture. To the right, there were open fields stretching all the way to Old Chester Road, obstructed only by 'The Oaklands' and 'Richmond Hill'. I have been unable to discover when 'The Acres' was built, who lived there, or even when it was demolished, but the houses in Acreville Road and Tudorville Road stand on the site of the old house.

THE VILLAGE, BEBINGTON, c. 1903

The transformation of the village over the years could be described as complete annihilation. From this view, all that remain are the Rose and Crown and Mayer Hall. The inn dates from the 1730s and stands on the site of a much older inn which is believed to date from the time of Elizabeth I. The high wall on the right surrounded Bebington Old Hall. The fountain in the centre was a gift to the village from Charles Hill who lived at 'The Oaklands'. It was erected in 1863, but removed to Mayer Park in 1905. How good it would be if the fountain could be replaced near the Civic Centre — a small part of our heritage would then be displayed for all to see.

BEBINGTON OLD HALL, c. 1911

The Hall stood at the junction of Heath Road and was built in the 1830s. It was used as the rectory for St. Andrew's Church. The first occupant was Robert Moseley Fielden followed by George Fielden. A visit to the Old Hall was one of the highlights of the year for the pupils of St. Andrew's Sunday School. After the present rectory was built in 1880, this Hall was used as council offices. In the 1950s, the Old Hall was demolished and the site cleared; there is now just a sloping grass bank that leads up to the new Town Hall. The roofs that are visible on the left belong to buildings in Heath Road.

ST. ANDREW'S CHURCH, BEBINGTON, c. 1903

This church merits a book of its own! One of the finest in Wirral, it has a particularly interesting history. It has been the pillar of religious education for almost a thousand years. Originally built of wood by the Saxons in the twelfth century, it was rebuilt in stone from Storeton quarry. In the fourteenth century, because of its colour, it was known as 'White Church'. Bebington's first school began in the belfry. When Cromwell's troops camped on Abbots Grange, they used the steeple for target practice. A poet, Robert Nixon, prophesied: 'if the ivy reaches the spire top all mankind will end'. The ivy was cut down and not allowed to reach the top!

Church Road (Stanton Estate) Bebington. N° A10.

'PAST AND PRESENT', CHURCH ROAD, BEBINGTON, c. 1937

When the Stanton Estate was built, it was considered to be the finest in Wirral. Three original residents — Mrs. Houlden, Mrs. Halfpenny and Mrs. Wright — still live here. In the centre of this view are St. Andrew's Church and Mersey Terrace. The cottage on the right, on the corner of Quarry Road East, housed the flagman who stopped the traffic when the quarry train crossed the road. Just to the right of this view is 'Edgeworth House', home of Lottie Dod (1871-1960). In 1887, aged 15, she won the Wimbledon Ladies title; in 1904, she was Golf Champion and, in 1908, she won an Olympic silver medal for archery. The house is now a residential home.

THE ROMAN ROAD, BEBINGTON, c. 1906

The Roman road, or to give its modern name, Kirket Lane, was created in the twelfth century, when it was used to transport stone from Storeton to build St. Andrew's Church. The lane continued to be used as a footpath and was probably also used by farmers to herd their cattle to the fields. No doubt it was also a favourite walk for courting couples! As with many places, time and progress took over and the lane disappeared — along with it went the open fields, Abbots Grange and a part of our history.

FOOTPATH TO Hr BEBINGTON ROAD.

FOOTPATH TO HIGHER BEBINGTON ROAD, c. 1920

The footpath ran from St. Andrew's School, across fields now covered by Tudorville Road and Acreville Road. The boy in the picture is standing almost where Pulford Road is today. From Higher Bebington Road, the path continued across more fields and through small wooded areas until it reached Teehey Lane. From there, one could carry on up Bracken Lane to Storeton Woods or turn left through fields and woods that are now covered by the Brackenwood estate. The houses in this picture are in Higher Bebington Road and were built in the 1890s. Most of the land on either side of this footpath, stretching from Heath Road to Town Lane, was owned by Major Orred.

KINGS YARD, HIGHER BEBINGTON, c. 1905

At the top of Town Lane today, there are a number of shops, including the Co-op. Long before these shops and Sunnybank were built, a row of terraced cottages stood on the land which was owned by the King family — hence the name. The Yard consisted of some twelve small cottages, mainly two-up and two-down, with outside toilets. A friend of mine, Wilf Willson, remembers the Yard very well. His grandmother lived there and used to take in laundry which was washed in a tub with a dolly peg. Some of the families who lived there were: the Everards, the Standings, the Prestons and the Jones family. It would have been a safe play area for these children.

CHRISTCHURCH, HIGHER BEBINGTON, c. 1905

The Church is situated on Kings Road. It was built of Storeton stone in 1857 on land donated by two brothers, George and Reverend Joshua King. The first vicar was George Troughton. In 1885, the bell tower was added. Visitors to the Church can see the fossil prints of Cheirotherium in the porch (see page 43). When the Church was built, there were very few houses in the area; just Higher Bebington Hall, Pear Tree Farm and three large houses down Kings Lane. In the early part of this century, there was a golf course at the rear of the Church; it extended from Town Lane almost to Kings Lane but closed in c. 1929. The fields shown here are now covered by houses.

OLD COTTAGE, HIGHER BEBINGTON, c. 1908

Known as 'Smailes Farm', this cottage stood on the corner of Village Road and Teehey Lane. It was the second house on the site and it is said that Cromwell once stayed at the original house for three nights. This house was built by Charles Inglefield in 1734. A large pear tree grew against the gable end — shown in blossom in this view. The tree was reputed to be 88-years-old and gave the house its name — Pear Tree Farm. The house was pulled down in the 1980s for road widening; the Acorn public house now stands on the site. Wilf Willson has happy memories of the farm and recalls that the farmer used to put the pig on the wall — to watch the band go by!

VICTORIA HALL, HIGHER BEBINGTON, c. 1906

The Hall stands in Village Road. It was built in 1897 to celebrate the Diamond Jubilee of Queen Victoria. The cost of construction was raised mainly by public donations. The inscription on the side wall reads: 'Te deum laudamus' — 'We praise thee O God'. When the Hall was opened, it was decorated with flags and bunting and there was a large party with a brass band. People could sit on the benches outside and gaze across fields to the River Mersey and beyond — without a hint of the dense housing that is everywhere today. The message on this postcard endorses this fact: 'I am having fine times; this is the place for health ...'

CHEIROTHERIUM, FOSSIL FOOTPRINTS

In 1838, when workers at the quarry in Scott's Wood were excavating some 60ft below the surface, they came across a layer of marl in which they discovered the prints of a species of prehistoric reptile. These are now known to be the only evidence that Cheirotherium existed — the name means 'hand creature'. It is disappointing that no other evidence, such as skeletal fragments or teeth, have been found, so it is impossible to deduce the creature's form. These footprints measure 8ins by 5ins and can be seen in the porch of Christchurch or in the main entrance of Victoria Hall.

THE GREAT CUTTING, c. 1910

The Great Cutting is aptly named. It was hewn out of solid rock, with pick and shovel, lubricated with the sweat of the navvies who dug it out. The cutting was the main entrance to the North Quarry and it was here that the Storeton tramway, opened on 15th August, 1838, entered the quarry. The large baulks of stone that were quarried, were transported by the tramway to the stone quay at Port Sunlight. Apart from some sleeper blocks set in to the wall on Mount Road, there is no trace of the line today. The cutting has been filled in, along with the quarry.

THE CROSS ROADS, HIGHER BEBINGTON, c. 1920

The picture shows Mount Road looking towards Brackenwood, with the Village Road junction on the left and Rest Hill Road to the right, but now shown here. The building on the left is The Travellers Rest public house, which is still there today. On the opposite corner, there is a small shop selling a wide range of goods; this is now a private house. The group of people standing beneath an ornate gas-lamp are simply posing for the cameraman. The area behind the photographer is Scott's Wood. In 1990, funds to purchase the woods were raised by the 'Friends of Storeton Woods'. The woods are now owned by the Woodland Trust.

STORETON QUARRIES, HIGHER BEBINGTON, c. 1905
The quarries were worked as far back as Roman times. In 1847, Mortimer described the area as: 'A range of hills crossing the township containing vast beds of the finest freestone, which affords employment to the many labourers who occupy the straggling huts and houses of the village'. The card shows the last quarry to be worked — its sheer depth is clear, as are the dangerous working conditions. George Green was the last man to work there. His final job was to send stone to Thornton Road, where a wall was built at the rear of a house. After almost 2,000 years of use in local buildings, that wall was probably the last structure to be built of Storeton stone.

Cottages at Higher Bebington.   Hugo Lang & Co. L.

BUTLERS FARM AND COTTAGES, HIGHER BEBINGTON, c. 1905

This tranquil setting is at Storeton Quarry. Butlers Farm ran the entire length of Bracken Lane; the row of white buildings, on the left, was their farm. Next, is the 'Little House', built in 1904, and now owned by Dave and Chris Broomfield; Chris being a granddaughter of the Butler family. On the right, are the Evans family's barn and cottage and, in the foreground, Johnsons cottages. Today, a modern house owned by Norman and Dora Boulton stands between the 'Little House' and the barn. Dora's father, Mr. Evans, once owned this part of the quarry. In the background, behind the trees, is Brackenwood House.

MOUNT ROAD, HIGHER BEBINGTON, c. 1908

Until the late 1920s, Mount Road was just a cart track, used mainly by farm and quarry traffic. The large outcrop of sandstone, incorporated into the wall in the centre, was removed by the council in the 1960s when the junction was improved. To the left of this view is Red Hill, where the famous 'wishing gate' once stood. The gate was used by courting couples who held hands over the gate and made a wish. From this point, views across the River Dee were interrupted by nothing but one's own thoughts. On the right is Bracken Lane. The roof is on the cottage that was owned by Mr. Evans; it is still there today. (see previous page)

NEEDWOOD FARM, HIGHER BEBINGTON, c. 1912

The farm stood at the present site of the seventh tee on Brackenwood Golf Course. The house was built of Storeton stone in c. 1865 and was owned by Lord Leverhulme. The land was last farmed by Billy Thomas. A map dated 1815 shows an inn called 'The Needles' on the site of the house. In the 1920s, Bebington Council acquired Brackenwood House and a large area of land which was laid out as a nine-hole golf course. In the 1970s, Wirral Borough Council acquired this farm and, after demolishing the house, added the land to the course, extending it to an eighteen-hole course. At the Bracken Lane end, there is still a small wooded area and park.

BRIMSTAGE, c. 1910

Brimstage, or to give its ancient name, 'Brunstath', was once the house of Brun, a Norse chief who settled in Wirral. The history of the village can be traced back for a thousand years. One of the original families to settle here was the Dounville or Domville family. In 1440, the ownership passed by marriage to the Troutbeck family whose residence, Brimstage Hall was built c. 1398. In 1908, Viscount Leverhulme owned the area. Not so long ago, the village had its own blacksmith and an inn called the Red Cat. Both have now gone, but Lord Leverhulme had the village hall built in their place. Lewis Carroll's grinning Cheshire Cat is supposedly based on the inn sign.

THE STORES, THORNTON HOUGH, c. 1908

On the turret, a stone bears the initials J. H. — Joseph Hirst. He built the shop and row of houses that continue down the road on the right. When this picture was taken, John Foulds ran the store — with its entrance in the tower — and the Post Office — the doorway where the people are standing. In 1923, the Post Office moved to its present position down the road, but the shop remained. The school, vicarage and church were also erected and endowed by Joseph Hirst. The school was built in 1866, in the grounds of the church; it still stands but has served as a Village Hall since a new school was built. This scene is almost unchanged today.

ALL SAINTS CHURCH AND VICARAGE, THORNTON HOUGH, c. 1908

In the fourteenth century, the village, known as 'Toristone', was owned by Roger de Thornton whose daughter married Richard de Hough; from this marriage came the name 'Thornton Hough'. Joseph Hirst of Huddersfield came to retire in this area. In 1867, he built the church which cost £7,000; the tower is unusual in that it has five clock faces. The higher, fifth clock was added because Mr. Hirst could not see the clock from his home, Thornton House. The extra face is on the opposite side to that seen in this view. On the left is the vicarage, also built by Mr. Hirst. Many village buildings were erected by the Lever estates. Thornton Manor is the Leverhulme home.

THE WHEATSHEAF INN, RABY, c. 1938

Raby is another Norse word which simply means 'boundary'. This village can be traced back to Domesday. In his 'Hundred of Wirral', Mortimer states 'Raby consists of 1,106 acres and is assessed at £1,220 with a population of 185 persons'. In 1801, there was a population of 131 persons, living in 22 houses. For almost 350 years, The Wheatsheaf Inn has been selling beer and offering rest to local people and travellers alike. The Inn, with its thatched roof, low beams and inglenook, has changed very little and 'The Thatch', as it is affectionately known, remains very popular with both local residents and visitors today.

RABY MERE, c. 1949

For older readers, the 'Mere' name must conjure up wonderful memories of long summer days: the walk from Spital crossroads carrying jam 'butties' wrapped in brown paper and a 'pop' bottle of water, hung around the shoulder by string. If we were lucky, we had a tanner in our pockets to pay for a boat ride and a Pendleton's ice-cream from Mrs Williamson's café — remembering to keep a penny for the bus fare home. However, we were often tempted to put it in a 'What the butler saw' machine, or have a last ride on the swing boats. I still visit Raby Mere, just to sit and recall those carefree days of youth. It is now a peaceful haven — not like this busy scene!

AN OUTING TO RABY MERE, 1914

This group were from Willmer Road Presbyterian Church, Birkenhead. In the 1900s, Raby Mere seemed to be as far from Birkenhead as Africa was — everyone had heard of it, but never been there. My mother told me that St. Paul's summer treat was a day at Raby Mere. All the local coal merchants would scrub their carts, place hay in the back, dress the carts with ribbons and flags and then transport the families to the Mere. The trip took an hour. Despite the dusty journey, these trippers seem to be dressed in their 'Sunday best'. The children did not have the freedom of today's youngsters who would surely be wearing jeans and T-shirts for such a day out!

DIBBINSDALE, BROMBOROUGH.

DIBBINSDALE BROMBOROUGH, c. 1908

The little bridge shown here is one of the oldest river crossings in Wirral. In Saxon times, the Mersey came as far as this point, forming a large mere — possibly giving the name Mereford or Marford. The bridge was known by this name for some time. On the rock at the bottom of the hill, it is still possible to see the wave marks that were made centuries ago. The bridge has survived, though not in its original form; some years ago, it was dismantled, the roadway was widened and the bridge rebuilt. At the top of the hill, there was once a castle or fortified hall belonging to the Lancelyn family, who came to the Wirral shortly after the Norman Conquest. In the sixteenth century, there was no male heir and, on the marriage of Elizabeth Lancelyn to Randle Greene the estate passed to the Greenes. The old castle has long since gone, but Poulton Hall was built in 1653 and the estate and Hall have remained in the Lancelyn-Greene family ever since.

DIBBINSDALE, BROMBOROUGH, c. 1907

This wonderful rural scene, in the very heart of Bebington, was captured by the local photographer, George Davies. George started taking pictures at the turn of the century, travelling around Wirral on a bicycle with his equipment strapped to a pannier on the back. Without these local photographers, we would not have such a comprehensive pictorial record of our recent past. This view shows a milkman or farmer delivering milk and could have been anywhere in England — fortunately, it is Bebington! The cottage still stands and is as charming today as when it was built. The road is a little wider but the trees and surrounding countryside are unchanged.

RUSTIC BRIDGE, BROMBOROUGH WOODS, c. 1904

The bridge spans the River Dibbin at the border of Marford Wood and Bromborough Wood — locally known as bluebell wood. The path and steps lead up to The Rake. From there, large herds of cows were brought down these especially-wide steps and led over the bridge to graze on the lush grass on the slopes of the Dibbin valley. I can remember the cows and farms in Bromborough Rake — also the pig pens and open fields. There was a long walk along The Rake to Bromborough Cross, to catch the No. 28 bus back to Rock Ferry — it is a happy memory. The name Rake is a Norse word and means 'sloping path to the fields'.

ALLPORT ROAD, BROMBOROUGH, c. 1913

After resting in Dibbinsdale, the route leads on to Allport Road. The rural tree-lined road, shown here, bears little resemblance to the built-up area that exists today. There were obviously some large houses behind these well-trimmed hedges but, unfortunately, I know little about them. However, where this road meets Allport Lane, there was a large house called 'Allports'. The village railway station is situated on this road and was probably the main stimulus for future residential development. Perhaps the message on the back of this postcard explains why so little is known: '…I would write only I have no news … nothing happens in the country'!

KNOCKALOE LODGE, BROMBOROUGH, c. 1910

This time, the name is not from the Norse but from the Gallic. It originates from the Isle of Man and means 'Kaelys Hill'. The house is in Bridle Road and dates from 1850. The first owner was Philip Quirk. In 1901, a Roman coin was found in the kitchen garden by Peter Calland — a copper denarius of the Vespasian era, 72-73 A.D. At one time, the house was used as a community centre. In 1959, the Associated Octel Company purchased the house and grounds and it is now a sports and social club for the firm's employees. The postcard shows the lodge to the house. This house still stands — a small piece of our history that is preserved.

PLYMYARD HOUSE, EASTHAM, c. 1970

The house occupied part of the site of an ancient abbey. It was built and owned by Edward Hodson Harrison, J. P., in c. 1885. This beautiful Elizabethan-style house stood at the end of a tree-lined drive. The entrance was guarded by two large gates and a keeper's lodge. The land around the house was extensively farmed, with both cattle and pigs. I remember the pig pens very well — they were along Bridle Road when it was just a farm track, long before the football pitches were laid out. Finally, the house was acquired by Bebington Council and part of it used as a chapel. In 1976, it was demolished by Wirral Borough Council; the site is now a tip for garden refuse.

EASTHAM VILLAGE, c. 1909

The card shows the Post Office with a sweet shop next door — this had once been a bakery. The Co-op acquired both shops and converted them into one. After World War 2, the Co-op. moved to bigger premises and Arthur Ferguson bought this shop. The clock surround is still on the wall but houses only a phone number. On the opposite corner is the Hooton Arms. In 1814, when it was just a farmhouse, it became a master's home for the school that was set up in a neighbouring ancient barn. This was draped in ivy and had a thatched roof — picturesque on the outside but inside was a different matter! In 1852, a new school opened and the master's home became the Hooton Arms.

CARLETT COTTAGES, c. 1956

When travelling down Ferry Road, one would have passed this row of white-washed cottages — just beyond the Hooton Arms. The cottages were built in the mid-nineteenth century. It is hard to believe that, sometimes, more than thirty coaches a day passed these cottages. The coaches carried goods and passengers, from as far away as Shrewsbury, to and from the ferry. Sadly, in 1956, the cottages were deemed unfit and dangerous and were demolished. The site is now a car park.

THE GREENWOOD TEA-ROOMS, FERRY ROAD, EASTHAM, c. 1908

These were a short walk from the ferry. The view shows the cottage tea-room where signs read: 'School treats catered for' and 'Private field for sports'. The small wooden shed was a shop selling refreshments, sweets and souvenirs. Along the fence, there are many slot machines and they seem to be well-patronised by young boys! The large shed provided shelter for cycles whilst their riders visited the pleasure grounds. In front of it, there are some 'What the butler saw' machines; a young boy is using one while his family wait for him. From 1910-30, the tea-rooms were owned by Jessie O'Brien who had another of the same name in Bebington Road, New Ferry.

EASTHAM FERRY, c. 1910
On the following few pages, I hope to illustrate how Eastham gained the title 'Richmond of the Mersey'. The first ferry boats were sailing boats — very inadequate and dangerous. In 1816, steam power was used with the introduction of the *Princess Charlotte* which sailed twice daily. Over the last 200 years, a number of different landing points have been used. This is because of tidal changes and the silting up of part of the river. In 1874, an iron pier was built to give a safer access to the boats. In this view, the building on the right was the ticket office. The ship is being guided by two tugs and was probably heading for the Manchester Ship Canal.

Eastham Pier.

EASTHAM PIER, c. 1910

The postcard shows the area in its heyday with many visitors on the benches and grassy banks. Three of the best-known ferry boats were the *Pearl, Ruby* and *Sapphire*. These were the last boats to be used. The *Sapphire* could complete the trip to Liverpool, against the tide, in forty minutes. She was the last boat to sail from Eastham. In 1901, a service to Rock Ferry was introduced; this lasted until 1914. The ferry finally closed in 1928 and all three boats were scrapped in 1929. The pier was demolished in 1935, but a short length has been rebuilt with sandstone blocks, and gives good views of shipping entering and leaving the Ship Canal.

Manchester Ship Canal, Eastham.

"The Unique Series"

MANCHESTER SHIP CANAL, EASTHAM, c. 1905

Without doubt, the Manchester Ship Canal is one of the finest feats of Victorian engineering. The first sod was cut by Lord Egerton in 1888. Two thousand navvies were employed in its construction. They worked and lived in atrocious conditions. Small shanty towns sprang up along the length of the Canal, where they lived with their families. In 1891, the lock-gates were opened allowing water to fill the 26ft-deep lock. Three months later, the 36-mile Canal was opened. This fine view shows the main entrance to the Canal, on the left. These ships are now replaced by modern tankers but, otherwise, the scene is little changed.

Eastham   Ferry Hotel and Entrance to Gardens

The Wrench Series No. 9638

THE FERRY HOTEL, EASTHAM, c. 1905

The Hotel, along with the Jubilee Arch, was the focal point of the area. It was here that the ships' captains spent the night whilst waiting for the tide and their turn to take their ship into the Canal. The Hotel was also very popular with day visitors who enjoyed their afternoon tea on the fine balcony. The Hotel was built by Sir William Stanley in 1845. In the 1970s, there were extensive alterations to the Hotel and the balcony was removed. In the centre is the Jubilee Arch, which was the entrance to the pleasure gardens beyond. There is a large group of visitors on the left — probably just off a boat — and many more can be seen through the arch.

THE JUBILEE ARCH, EASTHAM, c. 1911

The Arch was built in 1897, to commemorate Queen Victoria's Diamond Jubilee. It was the main entrance to the pleasure gardens which were considered to be the finest in the North West and were visited by thousands of people every year. The magnificent Arch had statues of Queen Victoria on either side; on the left, she is shown at the time of her Coronation and, on the right, at the time of her Diamond Jubilee. Above them, large plaques depict great military battles of her reign, and then there is a superb frieze of cherubs holding ornamental scrolls. Just visible in the archway are the ornate gates and the turnstile with a sign showing the entry fee — 3d. The posters advertise the treats to be found within — 'Ohmy's Circus' and the 'Topsy-Turvey passenger railway'. In 1930, the Council decreed that the Arch was unsafe and demolished it; when demolition was complete, it was found that the arch was as safe as the day it was built — what a waste!

THE PLEASURE GARDENS, EASTHAM, c. 1908

On entering the gardens, a world of adventure awaited visitors: lion and tiger pens, monkeys, the bear pit and birds from all over the world. In the woods, there were ice-cream kiosks and tea-rooms. Each twisting path led somewhere exciting or to a seat beside one of the beautiful ornamental fountains or to a quiet glade where one could sit and enjoy the natural beauty of the gardens. Just inside the entrance, there was dancing on one of the best ballroom floors in the area; it was made of elm and beech, with a bandstand at one end and illuminated at night. Although it is quiet now, the bear pit and dry fountains can still be seen in the woods.

THE CIRCUS RING, PLEASURE GARDENS, EASTHAM, c. 1910
This part of the gardens was used for live entertainment. There was a charge of 1/- for a ringside seat — it was cheaper to sit on the grass bank! There were various acts including pierrots, with their singing and dancing, the very popular performing bears and some circus acts. The brass band played morning, noon and night. Probably the most famous act to appear was Blondin, the tight-rope walker. He was a regular performer here and, on one occasion, pushed a young boy in a wheelbarrow along his tight-rope. Blondin was so impressed with the boy that he took him on tour with him. Blondin is most famous for his fearless walk across a tight-rope over Niagara Falls.

'LOOPING THE LOOP AT EASTHAM' c. 1909

Today, major theme parks advertise this sort of ride as the 'latest and best ever'. At the pleasure gardens, there was such a ride at the beginning of this century. My mother remembered it as the most exciting ride ever. It was called the Topsy-Turvey passenger railway. To begin with, there was a tall stairway to climb before sitting in an open car and being strapped in. The car then set off on a 200ft ride 'looping the loop' on the way and finally stopping at some buffers. My mother told me that after getting out of the little car, people would be shaking with fear and excitement! This postcard is one of many produced by another good local photographer — F Walker of Little Sutton. His work is easily recognised by the rather ornate lettering.

Eastham - Job's Ferry (1509).

JOB'S FERRY, EASTHAM, c. 1920

Job's Ferry is another name that is familiar to many people. Little is known of its history, but it was one of and probably the oldest, landing points in Eastham. The large stone blocks were, no doubt, cut and laid by monks many centuries ago. In 1934, the Bromborough Society discovered the old slip. Over the years the tide has taken its toll and most of the square sandstone blocks have been worn away or broken up. It is still possible to walk down the steps that are cut in to the cliff face, to see the remains of the slipway. It is a superb vantage point for watching the ships go by, and there are unbroken views of the northern banks of the Mersey.

EASTHAM WOODS, c. 1908
These ancient woods have many mighty oak and beech trees. It was once part of Wirral's vast forest. Over the centuries, its paths have been walked by the Britons, Romans, Saxons — and Victorians. The visitors from Liverpool called them 'bluebell land'. It is surprising that bluebells still bloom here after the armfuls that have been picked in the past! I hope that these last few pages have given some idea of the wonderful place that Eastham Ferry once was. In 1932, 70,802 acres of land, including the old pier and some foreshore rights, were purchased by Bebington Council from the Naylor Trust, at a cost of £17,000. The place then lost most of its charm. However, in 1970, it was designated as a Country Park and still has a lot to offer the visitor. Part of the pier has been restored and there are many paths in the woods, grassed open spaces and a nature and history trail.

MENDELL HOUSE, BROMBOROUGH, c. 1923

This large, imposing house, built in the mid-nineteenth century, stood near the junction of Village Road and the A41. During both World Wars, it was used as a hospital for wounded soldiers. It was then a convalescent home and this postcard was sent by a patient in 1923. He wrote: 'there are beautiful surroundings and the food is both good and plentiful'. The house was pulled down after World War 2. The site is occupied by Mendell Primary School, built in 1959, and Mendell Home, a residential home for the elderly, built in 1967. If all the demolished buildings of Bromborough were listed, they would fill a whole page of this book.

BROMBOROUGH VILLAGE, c. 1905

This was the main Chester Road, looking towards the Cross. Teams of six horses pulled mail and passenger coaches along this road, to and from Birkenhead. The row of whitewashed cottages had their front doors opening directly on to the road. It is believed that the row was demolished in 1931. On the left stood 'Cross Farm' which had the date 1699 above its door. The last farmer was a Mr. Kettlewell. The farmhouse was demolished in 1962, to make way for a petrol station. The tower of St. Barnabas Church can be seen in the centre. Built in 1864, it is the third building on the site. The first church was Saxon; the second, built in 1827, was like a large barn.

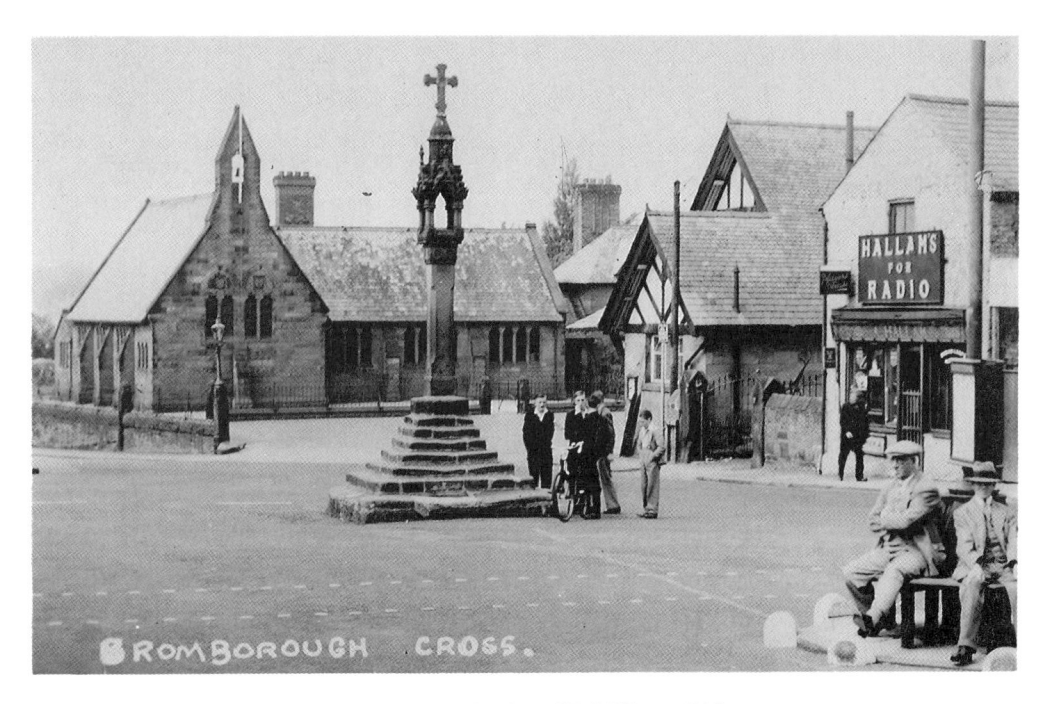

BROMBOROUGH CROSS, c. 1930
The base and steps of the market cross are of ancient origin but the top and shaft were added in 1874. A charter of 1278 permitted a weekly market and an annual fair to be held in June. It was thought that 'honest dealing would take place in the shadow of God's sign'. The cross is now surrounded by a small traffic island. In the background is the church school; one of the oldest buildings in the village. It was built in 1868 by Mr. Rankin of Bromborough Hall. The building is no longer used as a school. On the right, the men are sitting on the circular seat beneath the old lamp which was a popular meeting place, but is now the centre of a busy road junction.

VILLAGE ROAD, BROMBOROUGH, c. 1907

The white cottages at the end of the block were the oldest in the village, but were condemned and demolished in 1911. The fourth house from the left was built by Thomas Matheson as a reading and games room; for a while, this was the Chapel Coffee House — the words 'To him that loved us' can still be seen on the facade. The corner shop has a sign listing its services: stationer, newsagents, drapery, hosiery and millinery. The wrought-iron gates were a side entrance to the Church. Bromborough Hall stood behind the wall on the right. Today, this is a busy street with shops and offices on the left-hand side and a large D-I-Y supermarket on the right.

BROMBOROUGH HALL, c. 1909

The Hall was built in 1617, but was enlarged several times over the years and was, consequently, part Old English and part Georgian. The interior was spacious and rambling. Inside the entrance hall there was a stone staircase winding around the walls leading to a minstrel's gallery. On one occasion, workmen removed layers of wallpaper and plaster and discovered a priest's hole beneath. For many years the Hall was the residence of the Mainwaring family. The last occupant was Sir William Forwood, who moved here in 1898. Sir William was a founder of the Liverpool Overhead Railway. He also raised funds for the construction of Liverpool Cathedral.

BROMBOROUGH HALL, c. 1909

This is the rear of the Hall, with its walls draped with wistaria. On the right, the elegant conservatory appears to be filled with plants in bloom. An extract from Sir William Forwood's notes states: 'The gardens have an extent of about thirteen acres and contain probably the most extensive lawns and large trees in Wirral. The outlook across the Mersey is extensive and very lovely'. The well-kept lawns can be seen on the previous picture; this view shows flowerbeds and climbing plants, with part of the garden being laid out in the Dutch style. The Hall was demolished in 1932. At first, the land became a playground but the site is now occupied by a D-I-Y store.

STANHOPE HOUSE, SPITAL ROAD, BROMBOROUGH, c. 1910

The house stands on the corner of Mark Rake. Built in 1693, for the Spann family, it was known locally as 'Spann's Tenement'. After several changes of ownership, the house was presented to Bebington Council in 1937 by A. H. Boulton, a builder who had wanted to demolish it. The Bromborough Society had approached Mr. Boulton and the house was saved. In 1939, the Council opened it as a library. Again, in 1964, it was threatened with demolition. This time, the Society saved the house with the help of Mr. Richardson of Gawsworth Hall. Local fund raiser, Anne Anderson, had a collecting box made in the shape of the house. Today, the house is privately owned.

SPITAL ROAD, BROMBOROUGH, c. 1912

Most of these fine houses are still standing. One that has gone, and will be remembered by many people, was 'Heathfield' — once known as 'Heathstones'. It was a maternity hospital but was pulled down in 1977. The Summerfields housing estate has been built in its place. At the bottom of the hill is 'Sylvandale', once the home of the De Costa family. After World War 2, it served as the local Health and Social Security Office. It was then empty for some time, before it became the youth centre. In the grounds of 'Sylvandale' there is now a modern home for the mentally ill.

THE LODGE, WOODSLEE, SPITAL ROAD, BROMBOROUGH, c. 1920

The lodge stands at the entrance to Dibbinsdale Country Park — once the grounds of 'Woodslee'. The house and lodge were built in the 1850s by Mr Rankin as a wedding gift to his daughter. In the 1920s, when the house was owned by Sir Alan Brotherton, it was turned into flats for employees of his chemical works. A boy called Harold once lived here — his father, Mr. Wilson, worked for Brothertons. Harold went to Wirral Grammar School and eventually became Prime Minister. 'Woodslee' was demolished after World War 2, but the lodge remains. A path leads to St. Patrick's Well. The saint came to Wirral in 432 A.D. and blessed this well with healing properties.

DIBBIN BRIDGE, BROMBOROUGH, c. 1910

This lovely bridge once spanned the River Dibbin, close to where Otters Bridge now stands. I remember the bridge very well — as a boy I used to wonder how they bent the wood. It was not until later, when the bridge began to fall apart, that I realised that it was made of steel and cement! Brotherton Park and Dibbinsdale Nature Reserve cover an area of 47.5 hectares and are owned by Wirral Borough Council. The woods are part of the ancient forest of Wirral. An old poem states: 'From Blacon Point to Hilbree, a squirrel may leap from tree to tree' — the forest may have gone but the squirrels are still with us! The park is well worth a visit.

SPITAL DAM, BROMBOROUGH, c. 1950

Looking at this site today, it is hard to believe that there was once a thriving community here. A windmill was built in 1777 and stood to the left of the water-mill. In 1878, it was considered to be unsafe and was blown up. There was a water-mill on this site for many centuries, with a dam built to divert the flow of the River Dibbin. The large chimney stack, on the left, was erected in 1835 when Fawcett and Preston converted the water-mill to steam power. It was the last water-mill to be worked on the Wirral. The mill was owned by the Ellis family for many years, right up until its closure in 1940. It was demolished in 1959.

THE MAGAZINE SHIP, c. 1925

Magazine Village stood where McTays boatyard is today. It was built in the 1850s, by a London firm who made black gunpowder. The village consisted of fifteen houses for the families of their employees. The gunpowder was transported to the Mersey where it was stored in magazine ships moored in the Eastham channel. Three of the ships were: the *Liverpool*, the *Mersey* and the *Swallow*, the latter shown on this postcard. The land on which the village stood was on a 99-year lease. When the lease expired in 1952, the land reverted to Lever Brothers. The village slowly disappeared until nothing was left. The *Swallow* was broken up on the shore of the village.

BROMBOROUGH POOL SCHOOL, c. 1905

When Pool village was built in the 1850s, lessons took place in one of the houses and, later, in a factory building. Most of the time, the chaplain acted as teacher. In 1857, a school was built in York Street, with a headmistress, Miss Humble, and two assistants. By 1880, the school had over a hundred pupils. In January, 1899, a more modern school was opened with accommodation for 247 pupils. The old school was converted to a village hall — both are still in use. The card shows the boys' department; some are smartly dressed with Norfolk jackets, sailor collars — even a bow tie! Others are in an assortment of ill-fitting hand-me-downs and cloth caps.

87

BROMBOROUGH DOCK, c. 1987

Although the dock was not old in an historical sense, nevertheless, it has become a part of the past. The dock was opened in March, 1931. It had eighteen acres of deep water berthage, with 3,000 linear feet for mooring and 84,000 square yards of quay room. For many years, the dock provided work for many Wirral families and will be remembered fondly by people of the area. In 1987, the dock was closed to shipping and to all the small craft that were usually moored there.

The task of filling in the dock was soon started and, today, it is almost complete.

PORT SUNLIGHT, c. 1936

There is little that I can add to the many books that have already been written about this place. However, I felt that I should include at least one picture as it is within our area. In March, 1888, Mrs. Lever cut the first sod that was to transform an infested marsh area to the beautiful village that is seen today. It covers an area of 130 acres, on which stood 1,365 houses, school, church, public house, hospital, library, open-air baths, gymnasium, theatre and museum. This was before World War 2, things have changed a little since then. The multiview shows five well-known locations.

NEW CHESTER ROAD SCHOOL, NEW FERRY, 1990
In August, 1915, the school opened its doors for the education of children from the ages of five to thirteen. This lasted until the 1920s, when Grove Street school was opened to cater for children of primary school age. This school then became a secondary school, with separate entrances for boys and girls — and segregated playgrounds. In 1969, a new school was built in Higher Bebington Road. For a while, the new school was mainly for girls, with a small intake of first-year boys. In July, 1988, the old school closed and the boys transferred to the new school. This old building was demolished in February, 1991.

NEW CHESTER ROAD, NEW FERRY, c. 1913

Here, there was all manner of shops. On the right, there is Branch No. 5 of the Birkenhead & District Co-op.; Miss Helen Duke's fancy goods shop; John Porter, a hairdresser; Parks Cycles; John Price's stables and yard and the Primitive Methodist Mission Rooms. On the left, there was a joiner's shop; a fish dealer; J. Norbury, a confectioner; Lee Fong On, a laundry; a butcher's shop; a smallware dealer; a dairyman; the Post Office Sorting Office; a carter; a grocer and, at No. 100, Lillie Ellis, a confectioner. This shop was later to be run by Mrs Smith (see page 92).

With the exception of two or three shops on the top left, most are still standing.

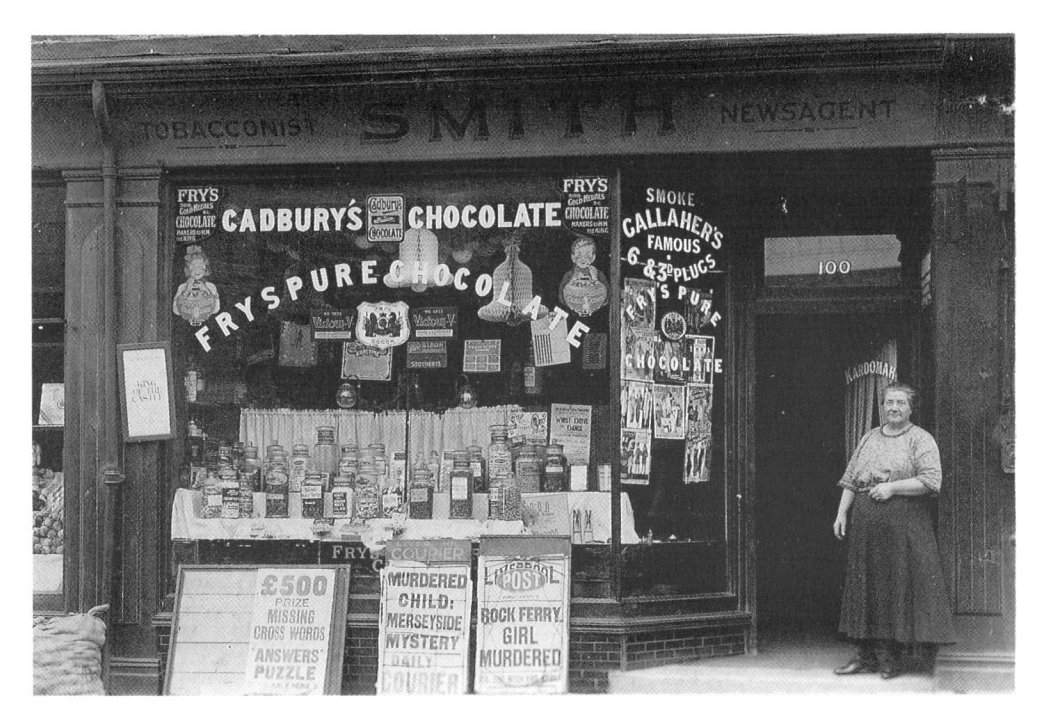

MRS. SMITH'S SHOP, 100, NEW CHESTER ROAD, NEW FERRY, January, 1926
Mrs. Smith is shown outside her shop with a window display full of goodies. There are advertisements for Cadbury's and Fry's chocolate; Gallaher's 3d. and 6d. plugs; Head and Nerve powders; Victory V and Rowntrees pastilles and clear gums. The glass jars contain all sorts of tempting sweets: peanut toffee, bonbons, butter creams, French nougat, Bassett's Allsorts — and bronchial pastilles! In front there are dishes of luxury toffees — rum and butter and brazil nut. Perhaps the most interesting item is the Liverpool Post placard: 'Rock Ferry Girl Murdered'. A policeman was accused but the case was not proved. The shop is now owned by Gerry and Dot Froggett.

THE TOLL BAR, NEW CHESTER ROAD, NEW FERRY, c. 1922

At long last, we are back in New Ferry — after a 25-mile trek around the old borough. Facing us is a very impressive building — Parr's Bank, built in 1901, and now the National Westminster Bank. It dominates the Toll Bar area. This picture was taken on the same day as the one on page 21 — the policeman is still on point duty and the group of men are still standing outside the Wynnstay.

The tram is at the terminus of its route which ran from here to Woodside.

I hope that you have enjoyed your tour and that, now and again, you will think of the history that we have lost over the last fifty years or so.

Also in the "Postcards From The Past" series:

Rock Ferry, New Ferry & Bebington

The Villages of Manchester

The Potteries, Vol 1

The Potteries, Vol 2

Newcastle -under-Lyme and District

Kidsgrove, Talke & Mow Cop

Stafford and District

Liverpool

Each book costs £6.95

We publish a wide range of leisure, local history and sports books, all of which are available from booksellers. In case of difficulty, or for a free catalogue, please contact: **SIGMA LEISURE, 1 SOUTH OAK LANE, WILMSLOW, CHESHIRE SK9 6AR.** Phone: 01625-531035; Fax: 01625-536800.
E-mail: sigma.press@zetnet.co.uk. Web site: http//www.sigmapress.co.uk
Credit card orders welcome. Please add £2 p&p to all orders.